GPJC
7/02

Explorers & Exploration

The Travels of
Samuel de Champlain

By Joanne Mattern
Illustrated by Patrick O'Brien

Raintree Steck-Vaughn Publishers

A Harcourt Company

Austin · New York
www.steck-vaughn.com

Published by Raintree Steck-Vaughn Publishers, an imprint of Steck-Vaughn Company

Library of Congress Cataloging-in-Publication Data
Mattern, Joanne
    Samuel de Champlain / by Joanne Mattern.
      p. cm—(Explorers and exploration)
    Includes index.
    ISBN 0-7398-1494-X
      1. Champlain, Samuel de, 1567-1635—Juvenile literature. 2. Explorers—America—Biography—Juvenile literature. 3. Explorers—France—Biography—Juvenile literature. 4. New France—Discovery and exploration—French—Juvenile literature. 5. America—Discovery and exploration—French—Juvenile literature. [1. Champlain, Samuel de, 1567-1635. 2. Explorers. 3. New France—Discovery and exploration. 4. America—Discovery and exploration—French.] I. Title. II. Series.

F1030.1 .M38 2000
971.01'13'092—dc21   00-041030
[B]

Printed in the United States of America
10 9 8 7 6 5 4 3 2 1 W 02 01 00

Produced by By George Productions, Inc.

Illustration Acknowledgments
Page 5, The New York Public Library; pp 6, 12-13, 19, 20, 22, 24-25, 26-27, 32-33, 40-41, North Wind Picture Archives.
All other artwork is by Patrick O'Brien.

Contents

Early Years, Early Adventures

By the early 1600s, many European nations laid claim to parts of North America. Some even had colonies there. A colony is an area that has been settled by people from another country and is ruled by that country. The land that is now eastern Canada was under the rule of France. It was known as New France.

Of all the French explorers who came to Canada, Samuel de Champlain was the one who worked the hardest to make Canada an important part of the French empire. Because of all that he did, Samuel de Champlain is known as the Father of New France.

Little is known about Champlain's early life. He was born sometime around 1567 in the French seaport of Brouage. His father was a sea captain. Even as a child, Champlain loved the sea. He once said that navigation "from my early age has won my love." Navigation is the science of getting ships from one place to another.

Samuel de Champlain

When Champlain was a young man, France was torn apart by the Wars of Religion. The country's Protestants and Catholics struggled for power and the right to practice their religion. Champlain fought on the side of the Catholics. He was involved in many battles on both land and sea. These battles taught Champlain how to fight. And they taught him how to survive without shelter, food, or water. These skills would help him during his years in Canada.

The Wars of Religion finally ended in 1598. The Catholics, led by King Henry IV, won. However, once the fighting was over, Champlain needed a new job. He went to see his uncle, who worked on a ship called the *Saint Julien*. Champlain's uncle got him a job on board, and soon the young man was on his way to Spain.

In the late 1500s, Spain had many settlements in North and South America. Shortly after the *Saint Julien* arrived in Spain, it joined a fleet of ships that were visiting those places. Champlain went along. In 1599, the *Saint Julien* crossed the Atlantic Ocean and landed in the harbor of what is now San Juan, Puerto Rico. Later, the ship traveled on to Mexico and Panama.

The Holy Wars, or Wars of Religion, were fought in France from 1562 to 1598.

Champlain and his shipmates returned to Spain more than two years later. Then Champlain went back to France. He gave King Henry IV a report of his travels, including maps and drawings that he had done. The king was so impressed by Champlain's work that he granted him a lifetime income. He also gave Champlain a noble title. From now on, the young man would be known as Samuel de Champlain.

King Henry wanted to know more about the New World, so he sent an expedition to Canada under the leadership of François Pont-Gravé. An expedition is a long journey made for a special reason. The king asked Champlain to join the group. The young explorer was thrilled to be part of the trip, and he and Pont-Gravé soon became great friends.

Canada and France

Other French explorers had already been to Canada by that time. In 1534, a French explorer named Jacques Cartier had visited Newfoundland and Labrador. A few years later, he sailed up the St. Lawrence River to what is now Montréal. Cartier's voyages gave France its claims to Canada.

Around that time, too, France began trading with Canada's peoples for furs. But France did not have any permanent settlements in Canada. The men who traded with the natives came to Canada in the summer and left in the fall. They did not build any storage areas or houses in Canada. They just camped out until they returned to France with furs and fish.

The French government knew that setting up a permanent colony in Canada would make the fur trade easier to run and more profitable. France would also be able to claim land and so expand its empire. With these ideas in mind, King Henry sent Champlain and Pont-Gravé to Canada.

On May 27, 1603, Champlain and Pont-Gravé landed at Tadoussac on the St. Lawrence River. This was where French fur traders came every summer. The Algonquin Indians were happy to see the French explorers, and invited them to meet their chief.

At this time, the Algonquins were having problems with a more powerful tribe, the Iroquois. The Algonquin chief asked the French soldiers to fight alongside his tribe if they and the Iroquois went to war. Champlain and Pont-Gravé knew that the Algonquins controlled the St. Lawrence River. Without their help, the French could not travel up the river to trade. Therefore, they made an agreement with the Algonquins, promising to help them fight against the Iroquois.

After the agreement, Champlain and Pont-Gravé explored farther up the St. Lawrence River. Before they reached what is now Montréal, they came to a stretch of water called the Lachine Rapids. A rapid is a place in a river where the water flows very fast over rocks. The Lachine Rapids were so dangerous that the French decided to turn back.

By the fall of 1603, Champlain and his companions were on their way back to France. Their trip to Canada had been a great success. Their ship carried a valuable load of furs, and they had found native peoples who agreed to trade with them over a long period of time.

An Iroquois mask and rattle

New Areas To Explore

King Henry IV was pleased when he heard Champlain's report about his Canadian travels. He allowed the explorer to publish his story. The work became very popular in France.

Champlain wanted to return to Canada, and he soon had his chance. Pierre du Gua, who was also known as Sieur de Monts, was a close friend of the king. He offered to pay for another trip to Canada. In return, de Monts would receive part of the money that came from the fur trade there. De Monts also hoped to start a permanent French colony in Canada. He hired Champlain to explore the coast and make maps. Champlain's friend Pont-Gravé was hired to command the ship. The group set out in spring 1604.

When they arrived in Canada, de Monts decided that St. Croix would be the perfect place for his new colony. This island is near today's border between Canada and Maine. Unfortunately, this turned out to be a bad place to settle. The island had little fresh water or food.

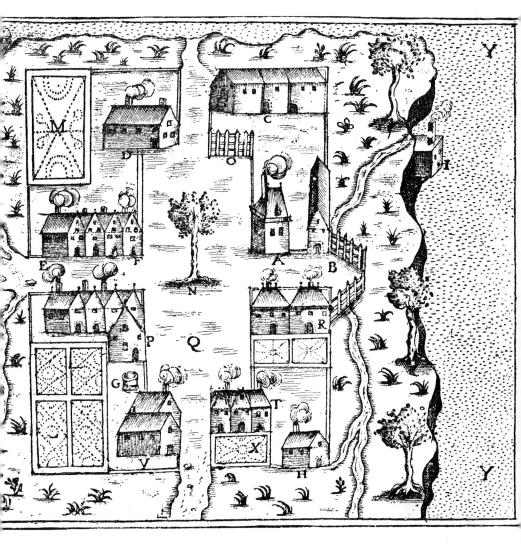

A map showing the buildings on St. Croix Island, where de
Monts and his men spent the winter of 1604–1605

Champlain's Four Voyages

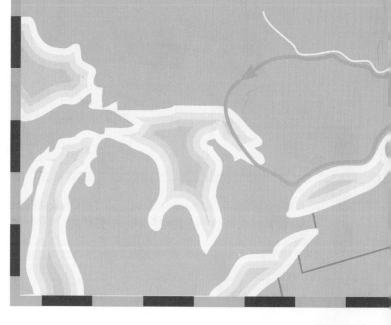

– – – – ➤ 1603

▬ ▬ ▬ ▬ ➤ 1604

•••••••••••➤ 1608

————➤ 1615

CANADA (NEW FRANCE)

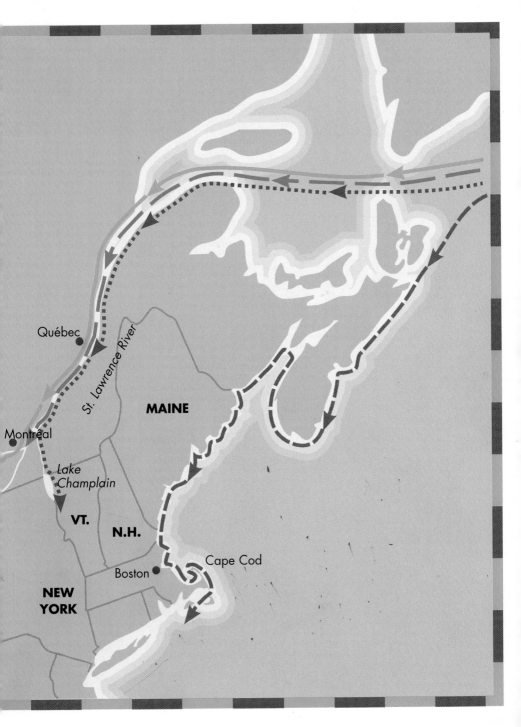

Québec

St. Lawrence River

MAINE

Montréal

Lake
Champlain

VT.

N.H.

Cape Cod

Boston

NEW
YORK

When winter arrived, deep snow covered the land, and huge chunks of ice blocked the waterway between the island and the mainland. The French were forced to live on a diet of salted meat and dried fish for several months. Without any fresh fruits or vegetables to eat, many became sick. Of the 79 men who spent the winter on St. Croix Island, 35 died.

In June 1605, ships from France arrived with supplies. Meanwhile, de Monts was eager to find a better location for his settlement. He set sail along the Atlantic coast.

Champlain and the other men spent the summer exploring sections of the coast of present-day Maine. Then they traveled farther south. On July 16, 1605, the explorers sailed up the Charles River past what is now Boston, Massachusetts. Next they sailed on to Cape Cod.

During their trip, the men saw many native peoples. But they had only a few furs to trade. De Monts decided to return to St. Croix Island.

De Monts knew his men could not survive another winter on the island. So he sent Champlain and Pont-Gravé to find a better place for them to live during the winter.

During the winter of 1604–1605 on St. Croix Island, 35 of de Monts men died from the lack of fresh fruits and vegetables.

The men traveled along the western coast of Nova Scotia and soon found a good spot. It was in the harbor of what is now Port Royal, near the present-day town of Annapolis Royal. Unlike the previous winter, the French stayed healthy.

In the spring, de Monts returned to France to find more soldiers for his settlement. Not many men were interested in going to faraway Canada. So de Monts returned with only a few people.

During the group's second winter in Port Royal, Champlain became friends with the local Micmac Indians. Champlain had a deep respect and liking for these people. He especially admired how they were able to survive in the wilderness so well. Unlike most European explorers, Champlain treated the natives as equals. He knew that a French colony could not last unless the French and the Micmacs worked together and lived in peace.

In return, the native people liked Champlain. They allowed him to take part in their ceremonies and helped him and the other settlers during hard times. Because the French and the Micmacs respected each other, it made things much easier for both peoples.

Sieur de Monts

A New Settlement and New Troubles

In April 1608, winter was over and Samual de Champlain sailed on his third expedition. De Monts gave Champlain and Pont-Gravé permission to sail up the St. Lawrence River. The two men found the perfect place for a lasting French colony. It was a clearing along the river surrounded by high cliffs.

On July 3, 1608, Champlain founded the settlement of Québec on this spot. It was the first lasting French colony in North America. It is now the city of Québec.

Champlain had a busy summer. He ordered his men to dig a moat around the settlement to protect it. He also had them build living quarters.

Québec was the first lasting European settlement in Canada.

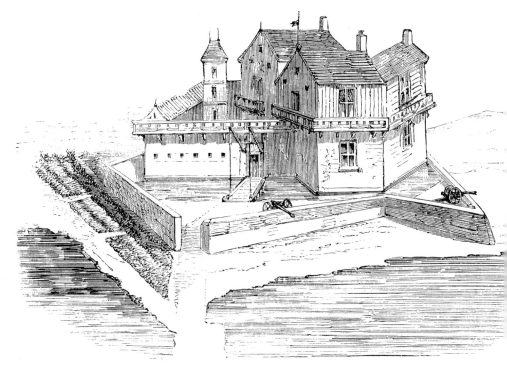

Champlain's fort in Québec

But there was trouble ahead. Although Champlain was a fair leader, some of the French workers did not want to follow his orders. Led by a man named Jean Duval, the workers plotted to kill Champlain and sell the fort to French traders from Tadoussac. Luckily, one of the workers felt guilty about betraying his leader and told Champlain all about the plot. Champlain quickly caught the plotters and put them on trial. Jean Duval was sentenced to death. The other men were sent back to France in chains.

The winter of 1608-1609 was a very harsh one. Of the 24 colonists, only 8 survived. Champlain got sick, but he recovered.

Champlain wanted New France to be made up of more than the tiny settlement of Québec. He knew Canada's wilderness was filled with valuable fur-bearing animals. And he wanted the French to settle the wilderness. To do this, he needed the help of the native people who lived nearby. So he made another agreement, this time with the chiefs of the Hurons and Algonquins.

On July 30, 1609, the Hurons and Algonquins continued fighting the Iroquois. The native people and their French allies, or friends, met the Iroquois at the spot that would later be called Fort Ticonderoga, New York. But a battle never took place. Before the fighting began, Champlain fired at the Iroquois, killing two Iroquois chiefs and seriously wounding a third. One of the French soldiers also fired at them. The Iroquois ran away in terror, and the battle was over before it began. But the Iroquois never forgave the French for these killings.

Then Champlain and his Indian allies traveled through what is now upper New York and Vermont. Along the way they came upon a beautiful lake. Today that lake is known as Lake Champlain. Then Champlain and the natives celebrated their victory with a great feast.

⋙

Lake Champlain

Good Times and Bad

During spring 1610, there was more trouble among the Algonquins, the Hurons, and the Iroquois. Champlain and his allies fought several battles against the Iroquois. During one fight, an arrow split the bottom of Champlain's ear and stuck in his neck. He pulled it out with his bare hands and kept fighting. This story spread among the natives. They admired Champlain's courage and loyalty.

The fighting among the native peoples became much worse in spring 1610.

In 1610, Champlain made a brief trip back to France. During this visit, he married Hélène Boulle, the daughter of one of the king's royal officials. Champlain was 43 years old, but his bride was only 12. Experts think that Champlain married her because he needed money to continue his exploring, and because she was very beautiful. Because Hélène was so young, she stayed in France with her parents when Champlain returned to Canada.

Champlain was back in Québec by spring 1611, but he didn't stay there long. Instead, he explored the area where the Ottawa and St. Lawrence rivers meet. Today, the city of Montréal is located there.

Champlain saw an island in the middle of the river. He decided to build a fort there to protect French settlers in the area. He named the island Île Sainte-Hélène after his wife. The new fort was to be called Place Royale.

Champlain and his men began building the fort. Soon after, he left to meet with his allies, the Hurons. After the French and the Hurons gave each other gifts, the Hurons agreed to allow a group of French soldiers to explore their territory. They also said the French could build forts and settlements there to help protect the Hurons against the Iroquois.

The Hurons went back to Québec with Champlain. When they reached the dangerous Lachine Rapids, they challenged Champlain to go over the rapids with them in a canoe. This was a compliment to Champlain's great courage. The explorer knew that going over the rapids could kill him—especially since he had never learned to swim! In spite of this, Champlain agreed. He became the first European to cross the Lachine Rapids.

Although Champlain wanted to stay in Canada, he knew the French settlements could not survive without money from France. So he went home to raise funds. By this time, de Monts had returned to France for good. But he now had new business partners who were not interested in giving money to keep the settlement of New France going. Champlain needed to get the money from someone else.

Champlain went to see France's new king, Louis XIII. The king introduced Champlain to Henri de Bourbon, the Prince of Condé and the new ruler of New France. Champlain convinced Condé to support a new trading company. Traders would have to buy a license, or permit, from the company in order to do business in Canada. The prince put Champlain in charge of the company. Champlain was now the leader of New France.

Despite Condé's funds, Champlain returned to Canada with only enough money to hire a few soldiers. There weren't enough men to build a lasting fort at Place Royale. Instead, Champlain took a group of French and a native guide with him to find a water route across Canada to the Pacific Ocean.

Many explorers had been looking for this route, known as the Northwest Passage, because it would be a shorter way for traders to get to Asia. What no one at the time knew was that the Northwest Passage didn't exist.

By the fall of 1613, Champlain was back in France again. He wrote his second book, which described his adventures in Canada. Champlain also raised money to get more men to come to the settlements in New France.

By the time Champlain returned to Québec in 1615, the Hurons and the Iroquois were in the middle of their yearly battle. To protect French business dealings in Canada, he joined the Hurons in their war against the Iroquois.

The way the Hurons prepared for battle was not what Champlain was used to. The natives had a great feast and celebration before going to war, and Champlain was angry at the delay.

The fur trade was important in Canada in the early 1600s.

Champlain and his men joined with the Hurons to fight the Iroquois.

Also, the Hurons sent only 500 warriors to join Champlain's group, even though they had promised to send more. On the way to the battle, the Hurons stopped to hunt. Champlain thought this was a waste of time.

In September, the French and the Hurons finally reached the Iroquois fort in upstate New York. However, during the battle that followed, the Huron warriors refused to follow his orders. The French and Hurons could not work together, and they finally retreated, or gave up and went back.

Champlain's legs had been injured by poisoned arrows during the fight, and he had to be carried from the battle in a basket strapped to the back of a Huron warrior. Champlain soon got better, but he was very embarrassed by his defeat. And his partnership with the Hurons had failed.

Champlain wanted to return to Québec. However, the Hurons insisted he and his men spend the winter with them. That way they would be able to plan future battles against the Iroquois. Champlain agreed. He used this time to explore more of Canada, traveling as far as the Great Lakes.

Champlain made several trips to France over the next few years. While there, he published his third book.

Champlain also tried to raise more money and find more men for New France. But the French government was not interested in helping him. By 1624, there were only 51 French people in Québec.

In 1620, Champlain brought his young wife, Hélène, back to Québec with him. But she was used to life in the busy city of Paris, and so was bored and unhappy in tiny Québec. She was also lonely, because Champlain was too busy with his work to pay much attention to her. Finally, in 1623, 25-year-old Hélène and Champlain returned to Paris. Champlain didn't return to Canada until 1626.

Final Voyages

In 1628, the French settlement of Québec was threatened by something besides lack of money and settlers. War broke out between France and Great Britain, and Canada became part of the fight. Six ships led by an Englishman named David Kirke sailed into Québec's harbor and told the settlement to surrender. Although he had little food and ammunition, Champlain refused to give up. Kirke decided the tiny French settlement was not worth fighting over and sailed away—for the present.

Shortly after Kirke left, Champlain received some good news. In France Cardinal Richelieu had formed a new company to rule Canada. Richelieu was the king's first minister and most important adviser. The company was called the Hundred Associates. Champlain was one of the members. Richelieu also sent supplies and 200 settlers to Québec.

However, David Kirke stopped the ships and stole all the supplies. Champlain and the colonists faced a terrible winter without ammunition and food. They had to eat eels, roots, and tree bark to survive.

On July 19, 1629, David Kirke and his younger brothers returned to Québec with three warships. Again they demanded Québec's surrender. This time, Champlain had to agree. His men were still weak and sick from the harsh winter, and they knew France could not help them. The Kirkes promised Champlain and his men safe passage to England, and then home to France. Sadly, Champlain had no choice but to agree.

When Champlain arrived in Plymouth, England, in October 1629, he received wonderful news. The war between France and Great Britain had ended in April—before Champlain had surrendered Québec to the Kirke brothers. That meant that Canada still belonged to France!

In 1632, King Charles I of England returned Canada to France. In exchange, France paid England a large sum of money. By May 1633, Champlain was back in Canada. He found Québec in ruins. Although he was in his mid-sixties, Champlain immediately began rebuilding the settlement.

In 1628, English ships sailed into Québec harbor and demanded that the French surrender.

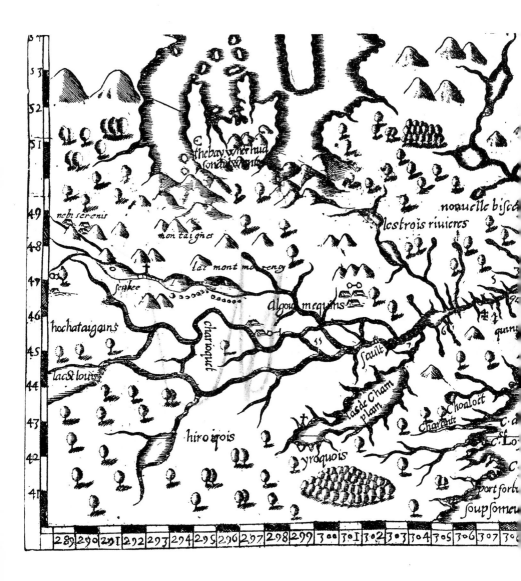

**New France as shown on part of Champlain's 1613 map.
The names are in French.**

By this time, Cardinal Richelieu had lost interest in Canada. He never sent Champlain the soldiers he had promised. However, in spite of this lack of

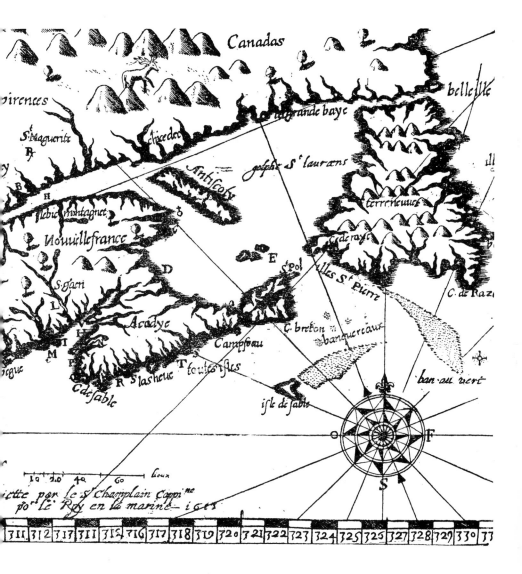

support, the fur trade between Canada and France continued to grow. More merchants and settlers came to live in New France. A new settlement was built between Québec and Montréal. At last, New France was beginning to thrive.

Samuel de Champlain is known as the Father of New France.

In October 1635, Champlain suffered a stroke. Weak and unable to move, he died in Québec two months later, on Christmas Day. Both French and native peoples mourned his death.

Champlain was a quiet hero, determined to see France prosper in the Americas. Through his hard work and adventurous spirit, the Father of New France saw his dream come true.

Other Events of
the 17th Century
(1601 – 1700)

During the century that Champlain was exploring North America, events were happening in other parts of the world. Some of these were:

1632   Italian scientist Galileo Galilei supports the idea that the sun, and not Earth, is the center of the solar system.

1642–1649   King Charles I of England and the country's parliament fight for leadership. The conflict is known as the English Civil War.

1643   The Taj Mahal, a building surrounded by gardens, is completed in India. Emperor Shah Jahan had it built in memory of his wife.

1644   Ch'ing Dynasty is established in China.

1652   Foundation of Cape Colony by the Dutch.

1659   French found trading station on Senegal coast of Africa.

Time Line

1567?	Samuel Champlain is born in Brouage, France.
1586–1598	Champlain fights on the side of the Catholics during France's Wars of Religion.
1599–1601	Champlain travels to Puerto Rico, Mexico, and Panama aboard the Spanish ship *Saint Julien.*
1603	Champlain sails to Canada to trade with the native peoples and establish a lasting French settlement.
1605–1606	Champlain visits present-day Maine, Boston, and Cape Cod.
July 3, 1608	Champlain and his friend François Pont-Gravé found Québec.
1609	Champlain and the French fight alongside the Algonquin and Hurons against the Iroquois. Champlain names Lake Champlain after himself.
1610	Champlain returns to France and marries 12-year-old Hélène Boulle.
1611	Champlain builds Place Royale at the site of present-day Montréal.
1611	The Prince of Condé is named leader of New France and starts a trading company. Champlain is put in charge of it and becomes the ruler of New France.

1615	French and Huron forces are defeated by the Iroquois in what is now upstate New York.
1616–1624	Champlain makes several trips to France in an unsuccessful effort to find money and settlers for Québec.
1620	Champlain's wife, Hélène, joins him in Canada but is very unhappy there.
1624	Hélène returns to France.
1628	Champlain refuses to surrender Québec to British forces led by David Kirke. France's Cardinal Richelieu forms the Hundred Associates to rule Canada and names Champlain as one of the Associates.
July 19, 1629	Champlain is forced to surrender Québec to the British.
1632	King Charles I of England returns Canada to France.
1632	Champlain returns to Québec to rebuild the settlement.
October 1635	Champlain suffers a stroke.
December 25, 1635	Champlain dies in Québec.

Glossary

Algonquins (al-GAHN-kwinz) A tribe of Native Americans who were allies of the French in North America

allies (AL-ize) People or nations that support one another

colony (KOL-uh-nee) An area that has been settled by people from another country and is ruled by that country

expedition (ek-spuh-DISH-uhn) A long journey for a special purpose

harbor A part of a body of water that is protected and deep enough for ships to anchor there

Hurons (HYUR-onz) A tribe of Native Americans who were allies of the French in North America

Iroquois (EER-uh-kwoi) A powerful tribe of Native Americans who fought with the French in North America

New France The name given to the land in North America that was under the control of France

Northwest Passage A sea route connecting the Atlantic and Pacific oceans along the northern coast of North America

St. Lawrence River (LAW-rens) A river in eastern Canada that flows from Lake Ontario into the Atlantic Ocean

settlement (SET-uhl-muhnt) A group of people who have left one place to live in another

treaty (TREE-tee) A formal agreement between two or more countries

Wars of Religion Wars between French Protestants and Catholics that took place during the late 1500s

Index